About the Author

Jaylene Hibbs's latest collection of poetry is filled with words that encapsulate the depths of her heart. Her poetry will dare you to walk into the parts of yourself that you forgot existed and will shine a light onto the magic that we all feel, yet cannot see. Her words are a glimpse into how she views the world – the beautiful, the ugly, the light and the dark. Jaylene currently resides on the Gold Coast – Australia. A place she will forever hold in her heart.

About the Illustrator – Mira Lou

From the moment I first saw Mira Lou's illustrations, I knew I had to connect with her. Her art is beautiful, soulful and captures magic within each line. Working with Mira Lou has been an effortless, magical and inspiring journey. Her art speaks a different kind of language, one that captures the essence of what it is to be human, softly surrendering to the magic of life.

Mira Lou can be found here
@miraalou
www.miraalou.com

Her Blue Lagoon Heart

Jaylene Hibbs

Her Blue Lagoon Heart

Olympia Publishers
London

www.olympiapublishers.com
OLYMPIA PAPERBACK EDITION

Copyright © Jaylene Hibbs 2024

The right of Jaylene Hibbs to be identified as author of
this work has been asserted in accordance with sections 77 and 78
of the Copyright, Designs and Patents Act 1988.

All Rights Reserved

No reproduction, copy or transmission of this publication
may be made without written permission.
No paragraph of this publication may be reproduced,
copied or transmitted save with the written permission of the
publisher, or in accordance with the provisions
of the Copyright Act 1956 (as amended).

Any person who commits any unauthorised act in relation to
this publication may be liable to criminal
prosecution and civil claims for damage.

A CIP catalogue record for this title is
available from the British Library.

ISBN: 978-1-80439-176-1

This is a work of fiction.
Names, characters, places and incidents originate from the writer's
imagination. Any resemblance to actual persons, living or dead, is
purely coincidental.

First Published in 2024

Olympia Publishers
Tallis House
2 Tallis Street
London
EC4Y 0AB

Printed in Great Britain

Dedication

For the day dreamers, who see with magic in their eyes
and walk with love in their heart.

A Note from the Author

This book was written during the quiet moments where the whispers of my heart could be heard. Words that were clear, murky and meant to be expressed in the only way that I know best to express, and so was birthed...

                        Her Blue Lagoon Heart.

The essence of these words hold so much depth and when given the space to live, will ignite spirit into your life as they have mine. I ask that you read this book with a sparkling wine in one hand and a heart full of love, open to hold space for what you are about to read. Be with this book the way you would be with your best friend. Give her all of your attention and listen to what she is telling you, for there is magic laced within her words. May your journey of life be as full as your glass.

Much love from my Blue Lagoon Heart to yours.

Jaylene Hibbs

Her Blue Lagoon Heart

Quiet words that slipped from her blue lagoon heart
to be heard, to be felt, to be read.

```
            T  h
                e

                  S
              n
           a
              k
                e
                  s
```

I'm finding that there are a lot of snakes in my
garden, and even though they like the soil
beneath their bellies – the sun on their skin.
It is not their home.
It is mine.

Inhale: adventure, love, courage.

Exhale: life was over.

                                                    Did you live a good life?

Sacred Conversations

"Has anyone told you how beautiful you look?"
she whispered to herself.

Self Talk

Baby, they're going to laugh, criticise, shame and steal from you...

But hold that fierce heart high and walk into that room anyway.

Yes you can
  – The heart

F.r.e.c.k.l.e.s

Have you ever thought that those freckles on your face are an eternal love affair with the sun?

He kissed her skin,
he never wanted to leave her.

Imagine a love like that.

Sweetheart,
you have a sweet heart.

You are allowed to change,
and change back again.
Don't let anyone tell you that you can't.
See darling, they're scared.
Not for you, for themselves.
See they have spent their whole lives living a lie.
Fitting in and acting a certain way.
And to find out the truth when you're at the end
of your life – is worse than death.

Beige

She hid herself.
She even ignored the shouts and screams coming from within.
She wore beige.
She lived beige.
She talked beige.
Until one day, she realised that life was too beautiful to waste on beige bullshit conversations.
So she drew rainbows on her hands, shaved her head, howled at the moon and never turned back.

She looked at her body
and decided it was perfect.

Life

She blinked and it was over.
She realised that she had spent her whole life
carrying the opinions of others.
A single tear fell from her eye.
That's all she allowed.
She decided right there,
that this magical life was hers.
Hers to do as she pleased.

She closed her eyes and left in peace.

Swaying – there is something so magical about it.

What if they didn't like her?
What if they made fun of her behind her back?
Or even worse,
to her face, disguised as a friendly joke.

She made mistakes, of course she did.
But that's why she was so good.
She had the courage to make them
and the patience to learn from them.

Imagine if you had the courage to live the life you always wanted.

Would it be worth it?

Don't stare.
Look.
Not with your eyes.
With that magnificent heart of yours.

T
H
E

O
N
E

She wandered about in her life
searching for the ONE.
Little did she know that the ONE,
that mysterious ONE she had searched for...

Was her all along.

His voice,
the remedy
to my broken heart.

Can you love?
I mean really truly love.
When the space is so vast that all you hear are echoes.
Could you still love?

Who cares what they think,
when what they think
are not their thoughts.

Breathe in that love.
Breathe it in deep.
Let it drench into you.
Let it saturate your soul
and drip from your body.
Let it leave traces
behind you as you walk.
Let that love become you,
so when people try to describe you

ALL THEY CAN THINK OF IS LOVE.

Broken – she sat in her chair.
Broken – she hated others.
Broken – she hid.
But beneath that broken, was a person craving love.

Don't compare me.
It's a game that will never be won.
It doesn't motivate me, it turns the
volume down and covers my mouth.
Don't compare me.
My magic is mine.
Their magic is theirs.

The voice in her head was loud.
It could be so mean,
especially when she wasn't paying attention.

(But oh could it be sweet when she did pay attention)

When she walked,
she left the scent of love
lingering behind her.
It was beautiful,
but it also brought the starving.
The ones that didn't have enough
love in them.
The ones that were deprived of
the love she so abundantly had.

So they tried to suck the love out of her,
like leeches upon her skin.

Shivers ran up my body making me shimmy.
I laughed because the universe just wanted to see me dance.

The relationship she had with herself was a love story that would be told years from now, like it was a made-up fairy tale between two lovers.

You don't belong to anyone.

>
> YOU
>
> ARE
>
> FREE

She laughed easily and smiled like a lighthouse.
Her flame attracted sailors from all seven seas.

She walked like a flower floating in the breeze.
And when she touched you,
the Earth stopped for a fraction of a second.

She spoke like a lullaby and those eyes, they were
big like the ocean calling you to swim with her.

She was irresistible and had no idea.

Fall in love with yourself.
Make it the greatest love affair of your life.

She placed her tired body
on the edge of her bed,
at the end of a very long day.
She removed her makeup,
pulled her hair down,
threw off her clothes
and sighed...

                    Is this all life can give?

The Mermaids

They swam into my life.
Kissed the wounds made by fierce storms.
Untangled the seaweed that restricted my breath.
They taught me what it was to be free.
They swam into the open waters, beckoning me to follow.

But I was not a mermaid.

Write a love letter to all of your friends.

If you don't feel comfortable,
what does that tell you about the people you
decide to call friends?

Sometimes she cried.
It was such a sweet surrender.
All those emotions she held,
were let to run free.

When the time comes. It comes.
Whether you are ready or not.
It takes courage to jump.

But
Jump
You
Must.

Fun, light, easy, bright.

– The mantra to a great life.

Change.
She felt it.
But could not see it.
Because some things in this life,
are meant only for the heart,
and not for the eyes.

She said goodbye.
She said good luck.
She said thank you.
She kissed her old life.
And danced open-armed,
into a new era.

Breath,
the love story of life.

She did a trust fall with the universe.

The potency of life
can either be
strong or weak.

Pour your cordial accordingly.

LONELINESS

the
medicine
she
needed
to
feel
full
again.

GROWTH

A love story
etched in other people's opinions.

She became very picky with the people she let in.
If you wanted to be her friend, you had to be real.
You had to love her in her beauty and in her ugly.
Stand with her in her light and in her dark.
Because life is full of highs and lows,
and she wasn't impressed with the surface level friends.
The ones that couldn't stick around
when things got tough and murky.
She wanted deep soul connections that shook her to her core,
lifted her up into her magic when she forgot who she was
and danced in her greatness.

The Vibes

She could feel them,
before a word was even uttered.

No response, is a response

.

.

.

.

.

.

.

.

.

*broken friendship

She had set the precedent to let others walk over her,
but she told herself it was okay.
That they loved her.
That they would never truly hurt her.

But their words that were disguised and drenched in
sarcasm, bitterness, shame and double standards...

Had stung her one too many times.

Stepping into ones power
is like giving birth to yourself.

— Painful yet liberating.

The eyes of beauty.
The lips of heaven.
The skin of God.

– Mirror gazing

You're a bird.
Your wings were created for you to fly.
Not to be tucked behind and kept at bay.
You are meant to see so much more.
Remember that the next time you go to
follow those chickens.

Wisdom

Your words are magic
and not meant for everyone.

Would you rather have one real friend or ten convenient friends?

Questions I ask myself daily.

The journey of life
will have you
looking at beauty
that you would never have imagined.

The girls that pull each other down.
Who laugh at each other.
Who gossip behind each other's backs.
They're not for me.

The women who have waded through their own messy shit
and have come out the other side.
Hearts full and arms outstretched.
They're the ones for me.

They're my people.

People pleasing – the art of not loving yourself.

Gossip – like poison to the soul.

Waves – they have the power
to wash away
the energetic cobwebs
of the soul.

Insecurities look like
gossip, lies, and unkind words.

What does it mean
when you express yourself,
in your truest most vulnerable version

– And your friends don't applaud?

It's easy to stand in my light
on a good sunny day.
But are you willing to stand in my dark
on a harsh stormy night?

Truth in actions

Speak
Kind
Words

And watch your world change.

Listening to the heart,
in a world of people who listen to their head.

Life's hardest balance

You know what's hard... to lose your friends.

You know what's harder... to lose yourself.

Honesty
is honestly
the most
honourable.

Bleeding
That sacred time when you have one foot in both worlds.

First you
are young.

Then after
some time,
you are
just young
at heart.

If everyone was doing it,
and you thought it to be wrong...

Would you still do it?

Sharing our most ugly stories is hard.
But when you do – you might just grow.

Friendship is like a garden.

When you leave it and
don't tend to it, it may
grow wayward with weeds that
pop up.

But when you look after it,
check in and help to pull
the weeds out that
sometimes grow.
You will have such a
beautiful garden.
One that many people will
admire and ask how you
kept it so beautiful after
all these years.

Cherish your friends.
Celebrate them.
Love them hard.

If you hear them gossip about others,
be sure to know they will gossip about you too.

I had a dream last night
that I was swimming,
with some beautiful translucent jellyfish.
They started to wrap their tentacles around me.
I felt so completely loved and held, until I felt the sting.
It was crippling and no-one was around to help me.

But then I realised that I wasn't asleep,
and those jellyfish were my friends.

She could only see the good in people.
It was her *gift*.
She saw it in everyone except herself.

She talks about vibes and drinks herbal tea.
She shows her skin to the sun, while feeling the earth beneath her feet.
You'll find her chanting on her yoga mat then laying on her couch.
You'll see her wearing the most expensive dress, while getting her hands dirty in the ground.
her hair changes like the wind and her eyes have seen things that are impossible to explain.
She holds her friends dear and speaks the colour of champagne.
She whispers to the moon and sings in her car.
She loves the ocean and hates wearing a bra.
She speaks too fast and sometimes not at all.
Mistakes are often made, closely followed by lessons learnt.
And all the while, she does this with that sweet smile of hers.
Because this was her life after all, and life never looked so well lived.

Or felt so beautiful.

I've met some women.
Some magical, powerful women
in this lifetime of mine.
Who have walked the path less travelled
and have all come to the same conclusion.
First it's scary to be seen.
Then you are seen.
And you don't give a fuck what they see
because what you see, is far more beautiful.

I'm not a surface level kind of gal.
No, I'm an all or nothing kind of gal.
I'm a jump in the deep end gal.
Walk through the fire gal.
Dance naked under the stars gal.
Express every emotion kind of gal.
But not everyone is ready for a gal like me.
No, some are still living on the surface.
Some are still trying to be perfect.
Some are just too scared to be real.

Am I choosing love?
Or am I choosing what others think of me?

*or am I confusing the two?

The
Br_eakdown

It happens right before the breakthrough.

My value does not come from you.
You might like to judge me.
Especially when in your eyes, I look different.
But your whispers and comments about me,
don't make you a better person.

Have you tried looking at it from a different angle?

Pause...
Then act.

Flowers in my hair, *always*.

I'm not afraid to be seen.

I've been through it all.

And yes I look a little messy.

A little burnt around the edges.

But I love me more than I love your opinion of me.

Follow suit or be shamed.
Are they the only options we still have?

The rebirth.
It's a dark time, filled with the echoes of
past versions of ourselves
calling us back...

                                                            But you must push on.

Shake off the old outdated beliefs,
and dance into the new ones.

Change so often
that no one can predict your life.

Not

Even

You

The bridge between the old and new,

is
meant
to
be
walked
slowly.

Celebrate yourself, always.

There's one language that we have all spoken,
for the briefest of times – in every corner of the world.
That language is soft, sweet and wrapped in so
much mystery.

– The baby babble

Trust.
I give it away easily.
But see, not everyone
has good intentions.
No.
Some people like to take your trust
and drown it slowly.
Leaving you feeling
dazed and confused.
Once that trust has gone,
you have nothing left
except for empty promises
and a hard lesson.

Witches were just women
who were seen as different.
They were women who were
feared for having a voice.
For speaking out.
For living an abundant life
full of knowledge with a deep
intuitive knowing.
These women were burned at
the stake for being seen.
These women were forced to
hide who they truly were.
These women were hated for
being themselves.

I think I am a witch.

When was the last
time that you let
yourself feel the
magic of rain touch
your skin?

When was the last
time you truly let it
soak in?

Because these days
all I see is people
running from it,
hiding from it.

Have you ever
thought how the rain
feels, seeing you
do that?

Naked

The feeling of expressing your thoughts, in the hope that it may resonate with someone.

Have you seen them?

Those groups of women who always
have something nice to say.
Who cheer for their friends and
love each other fully.
They sing and dance and always hold
each other up.
They speak with respect and deeply
care for one another.

Have you seen them?

You may not like me.
and that's okay.

Because I like me,
and that's what matters.

The Vault

A place to hold secrets.
But little did they know,
it held far more than that.
It held misinformation and lies
that manifested into bombs.

Perfectionism

People chase it like a pot of gold under a rainbow.
But unlike that pot of gold,
perfect doesn't exist.

The effort I put in,
compared to
the effort you put in.

*scales don't lie

The Flow-On Effect

when
you
give
women
enough
space
to
be
themselves
without
judgement
not
only
will
they
grow

but you will too.

She told me
that the mind and ego
are beautiful parts
of our human
experience.
But it's not until
you lean into
your heart space,
that you will feel full.

The way you speak about your friends
when they aren't there
says a lot about your friendship.

I will not dim my light,
because you like the dark.
I will not hide my body,
because you feel uncomfortable.
I will not shrink in conversation,
because what I say is different.

When you speak over someone in a conversation,
what you're actually saying is that
YOUR voice matters more than THEIRS.

And know that if this triggers you,
you're probably the person
who speaks over someone in a conversation.

They tried to play me, but
UNO!
They didn't know I was a wild card.

It came knocking on her door
as she was getting dressed for work.
Unannounced, it just waltzed in.
How grateful she was for that day.

— spirit

She bent backwards
and her heart cracked open.
From that day on,
she lived a life of pure love.

It gets better.
You will find yourself.
Sometimes mixed up in the wrong crowd.
Sometimes mixed up in the right crowd.
And you will learn to honour your thoughts,
for they have guided you.
And you will learn to honour your body,
for the places it takes you.
And you will learn to honour your voice,
for it is the most sacred form of medicine.

I remember feeling like it was the end.
I felt as if I had let too many people down.
I remember feeling hated by everyone,
but worse – I hated myself.
I thought about driving my car into that bridge.
I felt like ending it,
right then and there.
But someone whispered to me that night
"There is more than this, I promise."

And every time I drive past that spot,
I shiver – at the life I could have lost.

Her brain couldn't think inside the box.
She tried, because she thought
that she wanted to be like them.
But the more she tried,
the harder it got.
And the more obvious it was.
She wasn't a box thinker.
She wasn't even a shape thinker.

She was a FREE THINKER.

Let your light shine,
onto the worst parts of yourself.
So they may feel your love too.

She once let someone tell her,
that the magic of crystals wasn't real.

– The absurdity

A woman's naked body
is meant to be admired.
It's meant to be seen.
But here I am,
sitting in my clothes.

Women hold sacred stories deep within.
Generational stories that have been
passed down.
These stories hold potent energy that
has the power to shift your
perspective.

Once this woman told me that
in her opinion,
my breasts were small.
She said it like it was a bad thing.
Like I should be embarrassed.
It was a weird feeling,
being body shamed – by another woman.

I hope you never feel that.

How wild,
that some people
cannot feel
the magic
when it arrives.

I love those women who are so full of themselves.
So full of themselves, that they fill other women up too.

The Blessing In Disguise

Once I had this friend
who wasn't really a friend.
She lit fires with her secrets
and when the forest burnt down,
she didn't care.
She was confrontational
and on her best days, self-pitying.
She had me overthink everything I said,
stressing over the smallest of things.
She told my secrets to others
and talked about me behind my back.
She was a gas lighter.
Have you heard of those people?
They're good at hiding who they are
and even better at making you feel like shit.
She went out of her way to put me down.
The crazy thing is though,
I'm so grateful for that friendship.
Not because it was great,
but because it showed me...

What I truly didn't want in my life.

She woke up to a morning text.
Not the good type.
The type that was laced with confrontation
and letters that carried a heavy energy.

– Gossip gone wrong.

Mind Games

The narcissistic currency of little self-worth.

I called out a friend today.
What a magical conversation we had.
It was the most mature, loving conversation.
What a beautiful gift it was.
To be able to speak so openly with the ones you love,
and grow from our mistakes.

Not everything has to end in bitterness and hate.

We are programmed to react,
instead of reflect.
Thus ending more relationships than necessary.

Look me in the eyes,
and tell me what you told them.
Do you have the guts?
Of course you don't.
Because saying to me,
what you said to them – takes guts.
Something you don't have.

But I still love you.
Because I know that you are sad,
maybe even as sad as me.

I have succeeded many times,
and the first ones to pull me down
or gossip behind my back – are women.

Why do we do this to one another?

As I looked around the table,
I started to realise who my guests were.
It made me want to stand up
and leave immediately.

The only time she spoke to me,
was when she disagreed with me.
Every other time – she watched and stayed silent.

She whispered sweet nothings
into the ears of her plants
as they grew on her shelf.
Holding her most wild dreams
within their roots,
believing there was no other reality
than the stories she shared with them.

And oh how beautiful they bloomed.

Friendships change.
Friendships end.
Friendships evolve.
Be open, be easy and know when the season has changed.

It's one thing,
to say that you are my friend.
It's another,
to show me that you are my friend.

Inaction
in a time of action,
felt like betrayal.

...Girls...
Who thought they were women
but acted like children.

Show up.
As you.
As your beautiful imperfect self.
With mud on your face
and matted hair.
Show up,
and live that beautiful life of yours.

Listen to the birds.
They travel high
and can hear the whispers
of the world.

Write your feelings down
on a piece of paper.

BURN IT

Then let your worries float away.

Love those who hate you.
It's like the sting from ripping off a band-aid.
You don't want to do it,
but when you do...

You can see how much you have healed.

I don't get those girls
who openly hate on you.
Then invite you to celebrate their birthdays.

Success is infinite.
It never ends.
It blooms –
With every thought
you could ever think.

She spoke with fire and when people got burnt,
she had to lovingly remind them that it wasn't her
fault that they were standing too close to the flames.
And if they couldn't handle the heat,
it was their job to take a step back.
Not hers.

Break your own damn rules.

I had this lady tell me that if she let me,
she'd have to let everyone.
She made me feel like I didn't matter.
Like my needs weren't as important as the rules.
Then the next day she asked me for a favour,
and instead of saying the same thing to her –
I gave her what she wanted.
Because sometimes empathy is needed
and rules should be changed.

Lead by example

What if this is just the beginning
of something incredible?

I've had so many women pull me down,
but it hurts the most
when it comes from the women
you call your friends.

Today I went away.
I logged off.
I went in.
It was the rest my soul needed,
to survive this crazy world.

It's been a wild ride.
You've met some awesome people.
You've met some shitty people.
And then finally,

YOU MET YOURSELF

It's so much fun
watching your friends soar
and step into their brightest light.

I. Am. So. Here. For. It.

I'll always be that person
fiercely applauding her friends.
There's no room for silence
when your friends are shining.
Life is too short.

Celebrate them when you can.

Never let your heart feel bitter
for the chances that you didn't take.

And just like that,
she started accepting her magic.
She accepted that she was destined for more.
Far more than what she was living in.
So she packed her bags
and hitchhiked to the moon,
where she set up camp
and lived with the nomads of the universe.

The gentle breeze
that touched her face
carried a memory

- of how good it could be.

The Overflow

Fill yourself up!
All the way!
And spread that love everywhere,
especially onto those that don't have
love to give.
Let that love spill to those that would
rather see you fall,
who talk shit about you when you're not
there and are living from a place of
scarcity and lack.
They need it more than they know.
More than you probably know.

Plant your feet into the soil
and grow towards the stars.
That way you can explore this world
while grounding your soul to the earth.
Those roots will expand
and if you're lucky enough,
a little bee will find its way to you,
fall in love and spread your pollen
so that your gifts may multiply.

The slow life.
Yes that's what she craved.
You see, slow wasn't boring.
No, slow was more alive than anything.
It was dancing barefoot in the backyard.
It was the way the clothesline swayed,
softly in the summer night air.
It was the sound of the sea telling her its secrets.
It was holding hands with friends and lovers.
It was feeling the Earth breathe.

Yes, the slow life was what she craved more than anything.

She dreamed of a better tomorrow.
Visioned it!
Felt it in her grip!
Yet she questioned her worthiness for this life.
Who was she to dream something so sweet?

                 - Ponderings under the full moon

Words.
They hold so much magic.
Yes magic!
Think about it.

The words you choose,
literally create your life.

What if all those princesses actually saved themselves?
What if their stories had been changed?
What if instead of the prince coming to her rescue,
she decided that she would be the hero?
What if the real story was that she found herself,
and fell so deeply in love with the woman she was?

Golden

The colour of her soul.
It was so bright – she had no choice.
She danced with it.
Became one with it.
And off she soared,
on an adventure led by her soul.

She learnt to love her scars
for they kept her alive.
She learnt that her body's way of loving her,
was to seal those wounds up – leaving a scar in its wake.
For if they didn't scar, they would be open wounds
that would slowly infect her.
She learnt that her body survived everything
that came her way.

She became forever grateful,
for those scars that she carried on her body.

They didn't get her.
She was born to see things differently.
And to them, she was too different.
So they let her go.

The worst betrayal a woman can make to herself,
is to tear down another and feel proud about it.

When women gather,
magic happens.
In the form of sacred words
shared in trusted circles.

Being guided by the most beautiful women
who allowed me to be *me*.
A gift that I will forever be grateful for.

A gift to this planet.
She wore crystal rings and layered necklaces.
Her clothing draped effortlessly over her shoulders.
When she walked past you,
you could smell sandalwood and lavender.
And if you were lucky enough and looked really close,
when the sun hit just right...

You could see her magic.

Speak out about the injustices of your heart.
If you don't, how do you expect anything to change?

Have you ever felt proud of yourself?
The type of proud where you stand up and speak the truth
to your friend, to your neighbour, to your family.
The type of proud where you walk away knowing
that they will judge you for not agreeing with them.

But knowing – that you did the right thing.

There is something very important
about watching the sun rise and set,
I'm only just remembering.

She stood outside and let the wind
blow her hair in all directions.
She laughed at the absurdity
of being an adult and taking a precious moment,
to play like the child she once was.

She was so afraid to make a mistake,
that she stayed stagnant.
Until she realised,
that change was the most beautiful gift.
And if the cost of growth was to make a mistake...

Well then it was worth it, to make those messy beautiful mistakes.

She will never get the honour
of having my precious time,

ever again.

My Beautiful

If you sat with me
and gave me the time to be real with you,
you would see my beautiful.
But you don't have the time.
You're too busy,
trying to get someone to sit down
and see your beautiful.

May your eyes always see
the best in every situation.

Surviving < Thriving

She speaks in metaphors
and gifts the lessons of her soul to others.
She's gentle and loud.
The world's most beautiful contradiction.
She can smell the rain
and feel the vibration of the moon.
She believes in what you cannot see,
and knows of the wisdom that this world holds.
She's been here many lifetimes before,
and still chooses to come back.
She's fierce and ineffable.
You can't quite describe her,
because you will always miss the core of who she is.
Her essence is what brings you to her,
and her heart is what makes you stay.

They showed up to save face.
They showed up because they wanted to look like good people.
They showed up because if they didn't,
what would others say about them?
But then they left...
And the people that stayed were the ones that truly counted to her heart in the end.

QUALITY

OVER

QUANTITY

*remind yourself of this often

Kindness was the currency
that she valued more than money.
It was the type of energetical currency that said
"You are enough."
"You matter."
"You are valued."
And the people that understood this,
were truly the rich ones.

You can't break a woman like that.

And trust me – they've tried.
But her foundation was too strong.
It was built on love, courage and an
unwavering knowing of who she was.

You can't break a woman like that.

Don't be like the rest of them.
You have something in you that is more
important than looking cool and fitting in.

You have soul.
You have spirit.
You have integrity.
You have heart.

Courage in the question.
Expansion in the answer.
Understanding in the stillness.

She was learning that
others could only hold pieces of her.
But what she craved the most,
was for someone to hold all of her.

She was so pretty, it almost hid her ugly.

Trust your heart.
When it shouts to let them go.
Let them go.

You say you don't hold grudges,
but I see you carrying pain.
You say you don't hold grudges,
but I see you hurting others in vain.
You say you don't hold grudges,
but I see you closing off.
You say you don't hold grudges,
but this isn't a one-off.
You say you don't hold grudges,
but I can see your spirit change.
You say you don't hold grudges,
but I can feel it in our exchange.
You say you don't hold grudges,
but energy doesn't lie.
You say you don't hold grudges,
but I feel it in your delayed reply.
You say you don't hold grudges,
but your words don't match your energy.
You say you don't hold grudges,
but I think it's a big part of your identity.

She had seen enough.
She had heard the words.
She had felt it all.

This wasn't where she belonged – so she left.

Some people will be dedicated to misunderstanding you.
They won't want to sit in the fire with you,
and talk about what happened.
They will decide to turn their backs and walk away.

But don't fret my dear,
for it's a blessing in disguise.
They aren't meant for you. Nor you for them.
Yes it will be sad – so mourn it.
Mourn that relationship like it was a death.
Cry, rage and forgive.
Remember the good times,
then send them off on their journey with love.
Even if they don't wish it for you.
Send them off and allow space for your heart to heal.
Because you never know who is about to walk into your life.

Let your feelings bubble to the surface.
Feel it all.
The rage.
The hate.
The unjust of it all.
Do what needs to be done.

Only then will you find the medicine you crave.

She was art.
But the thing about art is,
it isn't celebrated or revered
until it's gone.

The only way to find your rhythm is to dance.
Dance with life.
Dance with grief.
Dance with love.
Dance with stillness.
Dance with yourself.
Just dance, that is the only way to find your rhythm.

It was her golden heart.
Her wide-eyed gaze.
The way she smiled.
How long she stayed.
The sound of her voice.
Her courageous words.
The colour of her hair.
Her beautiful curves.
The way she sat.
The time she woke.
The clothes she wore.
The way she wrote.
The food she ate.
The way she loved.
The stories she told.
Her gentle hug.

What I've come to realise,
is that those preaching love
and in the same breath pulling others down – even subtly.
Are not the people with integrity.

A hard yet obvious truth.

She thought the absolute world of everyone.
But when the time came to say goodbye,
it broke her heart into a million little pieces.

She always gave them the benefit of the doubt,
but not everyone had that gift.
In fact, some people even saw that gift as
a naiveté.
They scoffed and defended their judgements.
Telling her all of the reasons why they were
right to tear someone down.

She could never understand why some people
only ever wanted to see the bad in others.

A Word To The Wise

People make mistakes.
That's how we learn.
But the funny part is, the moment you make a
mistake, some people will hold it against you.
They brand you with that mistake.
They hold you to that mistake, hoping to see
you fall and flounder even more.
It's as if they thrive from pointing out your
mistakes, repeating them to you like daily
affirmations.

Stay away from these people.
They have pain in their heart that they are not
ready to feel just yet. So they will use this pain
against you, through your mistakes.

She had a hurricane heart
and earthy eyes.
Her feelings were deep,
too deep to hide.
So she would swim out in the ocean
to the bottom of the sea,
where she would scream out her lungs
until she felt free.

Don't waste your days playing the victim,
when you can play the victor.

Those who preach mental health,
yet leave their friends treading in the deep.

Obviously, said hindsight.

She danced on the edge of pain and love.
Some thought this was reckless,
others thought it was beautiful.
But really, it was how she coped – not having to feel either one.

Talk about your wildest dreams.
The ones that feel big and scary.
The ones that make your stomach flip.
Share your desires and speak your ideas to life.
They deserve to live too.

She wasn't yet hardened like most other people her age.
She was still excited over small things.

If you have good intentions,
and you lead with love –

Well, then you can never go wrong my dear.

If you continue to treat me like that,
don't be surprised when I leave.

She held me at an emotional gunpoint,
finger on the trigger.
She enjoyed this part the most,
it made her feel less bitter.

I watched this other person come out,
someone that I had never before met.
The whole thing made me sick to my stomach,
something I will never forget.

It was disgusting watching her thrive this way,
drunk on superiority.
I honestly thought she was kinder than this,
and that our friendship was a priority.

But upon reflection I could see the warnings,
I saw it day after day.
Another reminder to always listen to your heart,
and to never look the other way.

She finally pulled the trigger,
boasting about her victory.
It was only then that I understood,
how cruel some people can be.

Just like a river, my thoughts go on and on.
It's a journey filled with waterfalls, tides,
shallows and currents that are strong.

The colour of this river: bright blue, until it's dark brown.
Forcing me to be still, and watch the mud settle back down.

And when the river calms, all beauty can be heard.
It is then, only then – that I can hear the magic of this world.

So when you see me go quietly inwards,
please remember to be kind.
For I am in a deep journey on the river of my mind.

Rule 1: expect the best out of life.
Rule 2: chase your dreams like nothing can stop you.

Her sensitive heart,
was too much for others.
They found her too emotional,
and disregarded her feelings.

We are just a whole bunch of broken people,
helping each other to heal.

This season of her life,
was all about change.

She was growing and glowing.

I noticed something interesting.
She took hours to message back,
but every time I was around her – she checked her phone.

The way you treat people matters,
especially the small insignificant actions.
When you roll your eyes or cut them off,
you will see something start to happen.

People will distance themselves from you,
and create a bit more space.
Because you're clearly not the person
who will be kind through their mistakes.

Our friendship felt one-sided,
so I decided to let her message me first.

*I never heard from her again.

I simply switched the bottles,
giving her a taste of her own medicine.

I don't think she liked it,
the look on her face said it all.

She spat it out, turned cruel and cold.
She even caused a massive scene.

I don't understand though,
I only offered her what she offered me.

Silently witnessing life in all its glory.

Well yes, maybe I do feel a lot.
Maybe I do take things to heart.
But that is the way I was created.
To feel so deeply – is an art.

Metamorphosis

The colour of her eyes changed,
and the tone of her skin.
The length of her hair,
and the way she grinned.

Her choice in words changed,
her infectious laugh grew.
The way she held her body,
it was a love she never knew.

The friendships she made,
and the lovers she met.
She started to live
without any regrets.

This was her time,
a time of great power.
Where the petals of her heart
opened like a flower.

Little Love Notes from My Blue Lagoon Heart

To all of the magical humans who helped to bring my words Earthside.

Mum – for all of your support. Always and forever my favourite person.

For my many soul sisters who supported me every step of the way with your kindness, love and endless celebration. I see you, I appreciate you and I am forever grateful that you took the time to say a kind word and love on me.

To all those people who came into my life, gifted me with a lesson and continued to travel along their own path, thank you.

And...

To you the reader. Thank you for investing your time in this art. May the magical words written within these pages drift into your heart as they did mine. May these words set up camp and linger in your mind so they can speak to you as they spoke to me. May you feel the spirit of each letter, of each sentence, of each page. This book was created in a magical sequence of words that flowed through me, opened me, broke me and stitched me back together. Read this book from start to finish and then go back to the ones you loved. Mark them, fold them, draw on them – for they are the ones written for YOU.